# Drawing Closer To God

*A Study of Ruth*

by Ralph Mahoney & JoAnne Sekowsky

**Additional material by Doris Eaker**

**Aglow® Publications**

A Ministry of Women's Aglow Fellowship, Int'l.
P.O. Box 1548
Lynnwood, WA 98046-1548
USA

# AGLOW BIBLE STUDIES AND WORKBOOKS

## Basic Series

**God's Daughter**
*Practical Aspects of a Christian Woman's Life*

**God's Answer to Overeating**
*A Study of Scriptural Attitudes*

**Keys to Contentment**
*A Study of Philippians*

**Drawing Closer to God**
*A Study of Ruth*

**The Holy Spirit and His Gifts**
*A Study of the Spiritual Gifts*

**Coming Alive in the Spirit**
*The Spirit-Led Life*

**The Quickening Flame**
*A Scriptural Study of Revival*

**A New Commandment**
*Loving as Jesus Loved*

**God's Character**
*A Study of His Attributes*

**Making a Difference**
*The Power of Servant Love*

## Encourager Series

**When You Hurt**
*A Study of God's Comfort*

**Energize your Devotions**
*Five Ways That Work*

**Growing Up Strong**
*Principles of Christian Development*

## Enrichment Series

**Teach Us to Pray**
*A Study of the Scriptural Principles of Prayer*

**More Than Conquerors**
*The Christian's Spiritual Authority*

**Walk Out of Worry**
*The Way to an Anxiety-Free Life*

**First John**
*A Pattern for Christian Living*

**Choosing to Change**
*How to Acquire the Mind of Christ*

## Workbook Series

**Introduction to Praise**
*A New Look at the Old Discipline of Praise*

**Spiritual Warfare**
*Strategy for Winning*

**The Art of Being Single**
*How to Get the Best Out of Life*

**Building Better Relationships**
*How to Put Love into Action*

*Write for a free catalog.*

# Table of Contents

## Cover design by Ray Braun

Women's Aglow Fellowship, International is a non-denominational organization of Christian women. Our mission is to provide support, education, training and ministry opportunities to help women worldwide discover their true identity in Jesus Christ through the power of the Holy Spirit.

Aglow Publications is the publishing ministry of Women's Aglow Fellowship, International. Our publications are used to help women find a personal relationship with Jesus Christ, to enhance growth in their Christian experience, and help them recognize their roles and relationship according to scripture.

For more information about Women's Aglow Fellowship, please write to Women's Aglow Fellowship International, P.O. Box 1548, Lynnwood, WA 98046-1548, U.S.A. or call (206) 775-7282.

All references in this study are taken from the New American Standard Bible unless noted as follows: TLB (The Living Bible), TAB (The Amplified Bible), KJV (King James Version) or by the full title.

ISBN 0-930756-72-X

# Introduction

The book of Ruth has charmed readers for centuries. It contains all the elements of a good old-fashioned drama: pathos, loyalty, romance, suspense and it even ends on a "they lived happily ever after" note.

However, if we only see in this little book an Old Testament story of virtue triumphing against tremendous odds or a bit of romantic history, we miss one of the richest episodes in Scripture—what one writer has called, "a garden enclosed, a mine filled with the rarest and richest gems and rubies, a treasure of illuminating truths."

Although there are many valid approaches to this study, we have primarily followed Ralph Mahoney's (founder of World Missionary Assistance Plan) suggestion that the book of Ruth can be most fruitfully understood as a metaphor of the sinner's coming to the Lord and his growing relationship with Him.

In this study you will become well acquainted with the use of *types*. A *type* in the Bible is a person, thing or event that foreshadows something or someone else. By studying the *type* we gain a fuller understanding of the person or things which the *type* prefigures. The New Testament, directly and indirectly, makes use of *types* extensively. For example, when Jesus called Himself the "Bread of Life," He was comparing Himself with the manna given in the wilderness centuries before. As we study the giving of the manna, we learn much about Christ's giving of Himself as "Living Bread." The *type* is a picture given to teach us a lesson or provide a better understanding of a subject.

As you go through this study, you will see that all of the major characters and many of the events in this story serve as types in the Christian experience.

Before you begin, read the whole book of Ruth through several times, if necessary, until you are thoroughly familiar with the events of the story.

# Life in Moab

## Introduction

### Background

The book of Ruth, the eighth book of the Bible, is sandwiched in between Judges and 1 Samuel. Its story takes place during a very dark time in Israel's history when "everyone did what was right in his own eyes" (Judg. 21:25). Nevertheless, by the time we have finished our study, we will be very much aware that God through His Holy Spirit is always directly involved in the lives of those who, regardless of cost, will follow Him. This is a book of new hope, new beginnings.

### Settings

The principal setting of the story is Bethlehem in Judah. The literal meaning of Bethlehem is *house of bread.* Part of the action also takes place in the land of Moab, which lies east of Israel, separated from the Promised Land by the Jordan River. Today, it is the nation of Jordan.

### Cast of Characters

When Israelite children were born, their parents gave them names that had special significance, which, as a rule, everyone in the community understood. Here are the meanings of the names of the main characters in our cast.

| | |
|---|---|
| Elimelech | My God is King |
| Naomi | Pleasant |
| Mahlon | Sick |
| Chilion | Wasting away |
| Ruth | Satisfied |
| Boaz | In him is strength |

*Prayer: Lord, open our spiritual eyes and our hearts so we may truly learn what You would teach us through this study.*

## Bible Study

Read **Ruth 1:1-4.**
(1) How was Israel ruled? _____

The judges functioned both as priests and rulers or kings during this time, although they had neither title.

(2)   What major problem did Israel face?_____

There was a famine—no bread in the "house of bread." This was part of the curse God had warned the Israelites would befall them if they were disobedient to His laws (Deut. 28:15-19).

(3)   How did Elimelech and Naomi react?_____

_____

Leaving Judah was a serious breach of faith for this couple. Many of the promises which God had given the Israelites at the time they entered the Promised Land were tied to their remaining in the land. Elimelech, in particular, whose name we remember means, "My God is King," made a mockery of his name's meaning by seeking relief from the famine in a heathen nation. Although Elimelech and Naomi were Ephrathites, meaning "fruitful," they were far from *being* "fruitful." Turning their backs on the Promised Land God had given to their ancestors, they took refuge in the land of Moab, which is a *type* of the world. Elimelech and Naomi must have been discouraged for some time before leaving the land of Israel, for they had named their sons, born there, "Sick" and "Wasting Away," rather than names with jubilant faith-filled meanings. The names reflected their discouragement and their lack of faith in God. In a time of Israel's chastening, instead of trusting God and seeking His face, this family turned its eyes to the green, fertile fields of Moab.

The Moabites were well known for their pagan practices, and historically, whenever the Moabites and the Israelites mixed, Israel sinned. Moab, himself, was the son born of the incestuous union between Lot and his elder daughter (Gen. 19:37). Later, when Moab had become a nation, and the children of Israel were returning to the Promised Land from Egypt, Moses asked permission to take the people through the land of Moab, a direct route into Israel. But the King of Moab refused to let them pass through and for that, the Lord instructed the Israelites to treat Moab with coldness and indifference (Deut. 23:3-4). The king of Moab had also sent the prophet, Balaam, to curse them (Num. 22).

Moab was an evil land, filled with evil practices. Especially repellent to the God-fearing Israelites were the worship ceremonies made to the Moab god, Chemosh, which included the sacrifice of children as burnt offerings.

Early in the time of the judges, Eglon, King of Moab, invaded Israel and established his seat of government at Jericho. From there he oppressed the Israelites of the hill country for 18 years until he was assassinated. In the battle which followed, 10,000 Moabites lost their lives and Israel reigned over Moab for the next 80 years.

It was during this period of time that Elimelech and Naomi fled "the house of bread" and went to sojourn with ancient, evil enemies in a hostile land. Elimelech undoubtedly was convinced he was doing the best thing for his family, but when we look to sources other than God, we will always end up in trouble.

**Discussion Question:** Many Christians have their "land of Moab" to which they turn when "the going gets rough," when their Christianity does not bring the "results" they expect. Is there a Moab in your life—some non-Christian activity or behavior you turn to when you are dissatisfied with the Christian life?

(4) What word in verse 1 indicates that Elimelech and Naomi thought of their move as temporary?_____

(5) What words in verse 2 indicate that their stay became permanent?_____

(6) What was the first tragedy that happened to the family during their stay in Moab?_____

_____

(7) How long did they stay there?_____

(8) What happened to the two young men (v. 4)?_____

_____

Sin can only breed more sin. Naomi and Elimelech, who had planned to only "sojourn" in this heathen nation, now reaped the fruit of their transgression—their sons married heathen women. Intermarriage with pagans was a sin according to Mosaic law.

**Discussion Question:** Can you think of other instances in the Bible in which sin created the opportunity for further sin?

Read **Deuteronomy 7:3-4.**
(9) Why had God forbidden such unions?_____

_____

Read **2 Corinthians 6:14.**
(10) What is Paul's command to Christians?_____

_____

(11) Why is this forbidden?_____

_____

History and experience bear out the wisdom of God's commandments. Seldom does the non-believer in the relationship turn to God; usually he or she turns the believer's heart away from the Lord.

**Discussion Question:** Why is this usually so?

Read **Ruth 1:5-6.**
(12)  What happened to Mahlon and Chilion (v. 5)?_____
    We can imagine Naomi's grief and sense of hopelessness at this time, but though she had left God and His provision for her, God had not forgotten her.
    Naomi had reached a crisis place in her life. After having left the land of her birth in disobedience to God and spending ten years in a heathen nation, she now found herself bereft of everything she had brought with her.
    Many people who have turned their backs on God find themselves in this position. The next step they take may very well determine their future and eternal destiny.

(13)  What news did Naomi hear?_____

(14)  What did she decide to do?_____
    Naomi had no way of knowing at the time, but she had just taken the first step on the right path. The decision to return home would eventually lead her to a happy and fulfilled future.
    In a very real sense, Naomi could be considered the "prodigal daughter" of the Old Testament.

Read **Luke 15:11-32.**
    Write out the points of similarity between Naomi and the prodigal son.

| Naomi | Prodigal Son |
|-------|--------------|
| _____ | _____ |
| _____ | _____ |
| _____ | _____ |
| _____ | _____ |
| _____ | _____ |
| _____ | _____ |
| _____ | _____ |

**Personal Application:** Perhaps like Naomi you once walked closely with the Lord, but somehow strayed away. If this is your story, why don't you tell God you are now ready to begin the journey back to Him. Yours can be a much shorter walk than either Naomi or the prodigal son had to take. All you have to do is ask the Lord's forgiveness and then determine in your heart to be obedient to Him today and in the future.

## To Memorize:

*Then she arose with her daughters-in-law that she might return from the land of Moab, for she had heard in the land of Moab that the Lord had visited His people in giving them food (Ruth 1:6).*

# The Return

## Introduction

Once again, there was bread in the house of Israel! The famine was over. In our first lesson we saw the sad consequences that resulted from Naomi and Elimelech's "sojourn" in the land of Moab and how after the death of Elimelech and her two sons, Naomi finally decided to return home.

*Prayer: Lord, breathe Your life into this lesson today, so we may fully understand what You have to teach us from the story of Ruth.*

## Bible Study

Read **Ruth 1:7-13.**
(1)  Who went with Naomi?_____

(2)  What did the two women do when Naomi tried to send them

home? _____

_____

(3)  What were Naomi objections?_____

_____

_____

According to Jewish custom, property and other family rights were passed down from father to son. Because of this, the law of Moses had established that if a married man died without an heir, his brother should marry the widow, and any offspring would then be considered heirs of the dead man (Deut. 25:5). This was known as *levirate* (brother-in-law) marriage. Naomi was referring to this practice in her answer to her daughters-in-law.

Her discouraging answer also reminds us of what Jesus said to many who mistakenly believed they wanted to follow Him.

Read **Matthew 8:19-20** and **Luke 9:57-62.**
(4)  What was Jesus' response to each of these:

The scribe?_____

The disciple?_____

_____

The other disciple?_____

_____

It has been suggested by some that Jesus is not nearly not as quick to *accept* disciples as we are to *make* them. Christians who at the first sign of trouble or hardship turn away from Him, bring Him no honor.

**Discussion Question:** What kinds of things stand in people's way of full commitment to the Lord?

**Personal Question:** Is there anything—a person, an object, action, or attitude that stands in the way of your full commitment to the Lord? If you have not already done so, are you willing to put the Lord first in your life—ahead of everyone and everything else?

Naomi had no illusions as to what life would be like for three impoverished widows, two of them aliens and heathens.

Read **Ruth 1:14-19.**
(5)    What was the response of the two young women?_____

_____

_____

_____

Orpah is a type of the person who hears the word of salvation but is not willing to pay the price necessary to follow the Lord. Taking Naomi's advice, she returned to her own people. However, Ruth "clung" to Naomi.
(6)    When Naomi urged Ruth to follow Orpah, what was Ruth's response? _____

_____

_____

_____

Ruth's declaration silenced Naomi's objections as she realized the strength and firmness of Ruth's commitment. Ruth had considered the cost and was willing to pay it. Although Ruth's words are sometimes used as a romantic part of wedding ceremonies today, her declaration was more than sentiment. It was a complete commitment to her mother-in-law and to Naomi's God. By going with Naomi, Ruth was willing to close the door to her past forever.

**Discussion Question:** Why do you think Ruth was willing to make such a commitment?

We have no way of knowing how much Naomi had spoken to her daughters-in-law of her God. However, the witness of Naomi's life must have been such that Ruth was completely willing to throw in her lot with this older woman. Remember, at this point, as far as Ruth knew, Naomi had nothing to offer her except poverty and hardship, but there was something about the older woman that compelled Ruth to follow her. Although Ruth believed she was following Naomi, she was actually being drawn to God by the Holy Spirit.

"Your God will be my God." With this declaration, Ruth announced her intention to forever align herself with the Jewish people and their God. In doing so, she serves as a type of every Christian who determines to follow Christ at all costs.

At the beginning of this study, we said that the book of Ruth can be considered a metaphor of a growing relationship with the Lord. At this point, if we were to use the language of the New Testament, we would say that Ruth was "saved" in the redemptive sense of the word. With her commitment, "Your God shall be my God," she entered into a covenant relationship and a covenant blessing with the Lord.

Later in the book, Boaz says to Ruth, "The Lord reward your work and your wages be full from the Lord, the God of Israel under whose wing you have come to seek refuge" (2:12). When Ruth made her commitment she turned to Israel's God and put her full trust in Him. This trust, coupled with the approved sacrifices for sin, brought salvation to her. In a similar way, we are saved by putting our trust and confidence in the finished, sacrificial work of Christ at Calvary. Jesus, the perfect sacrificial Lamb of God paid once and for all for our salvation.

Perhaps you, like Ruth, have frequently heard about the Christ whom Christians worship, but you have never really asked Him to be your Savior and Lord. Perhaps you know in your heart that this is what you want to do. Before you do, however, we ask that you, like Ruth, fully consider the cost. Jesus is unlike other masters, who may be satisfied to have you live by a set of external rules. Jesus demands your heart, soul, life, your all.

Now if you still want Him to be Lord of your life, tell Him so. Accepting Jesus does not have to be a complicated matter. Simply tell Him you believe that He is God, that He came to earth in human form, that He died to pay the price for your sins and was raised from the dead. Then tell Him you want Him to be master of your life.

If you have taken the above steps, you are now a child of God. His Holy Spirit is within you to guide and lead you. When the Holy Spirit speaks to you about sin, be quick to ask God to forgive you, and He will. Then determine not to commit those sins again.

As a new babe in Christ, you will need good teaching. The leader of your study group (or a Christian friend, if you are studying alone) will be glad to recommend Christian literature and suggest a church to you.

**Personal Question:** As Christians we, like Ruth, should be willing to put our past lives behind us. Is there some area in your past that you have been unwilling or unable to put behind you? We are not necessarily referring to "sin"; some people continue to feel guilt over their past, even after the Lord has wiped the slate clean. Jesus referred to salvation as being "born again." In the spiritual realm, you become a completely new person at salvation. How can you follow Ruth's example and put your past behind?

Read **Ruth 1:19.**

The Bible gives us no details of the journey back to Bethlehem. We know it could not have been easy—two women, alone, with only a few possessions, slowly making their way back to the "house of bread."

(7)    What does the Bible say about their return?_____

_____

The root of the Hebrew word for *stirred* means to make an uproar.

**Discussion Question:** Why do you think the people of Bethlehem would be in an uproar over the return of Naomi?

(8)    What did the women ask?_____
The ten years in Moab had not been kind to Naomi. She was so changed that old friends who had known her since childhood were unsure of her identity.

Read **Ruth 1:20-21.**
(9)    How did Naomi answer?_____

_____

*Mara* means *bitter*. Naomi—the "pleasant" woman—had returned to Bethlehem as the "bitter" one.
(10)   Who did Naomi blame for her troubles?_____
Here in these two verses Naomi bitterly laid a four-fold charge against God.
(11)   List her four complaints.

        1._____

2. _____

3. _____

4. _____

How human it is to go our own way and then blame God for the consequences. Any form of self-pity says in effect, "God could have done something in the circumstances of my life, but didn't." This attitude builds a wall between us and God and keeps us distant from Him.

**Personal Question:** Can you think of a situation in your life that has been caused through your own actions or sin, for which you are blaming God? What will you do about it?

Read **Hebrews 12:15.**
(12)   What two things does bitterness do?_____

_____

Read **Exodus 15:22-26.**
(13)   What was wrong with the water at Marah?_____

(14)   What did Moses do?_____

(15)   What did the Lord show him?_____

_____

The "tree" which sweetens the bitter waters in our lives is Jesus. He is always ready to come to our aid when we reach those places of bitterness. Through His power in our lives we can refuse to give bitterness any opportunity to establish roots in our lives.

(16)   What great claim does God make in verse 26?_____

_____

Not only can Jesus help us keep bitterness from entering our lives, but He can also heal us of any bitterness that is already there.

**Personal Question:** Will you take time to look at your life? Is there any bitterness? Are you willing to be healed? If you are, tell Jesus right now.
(17)   How did Naomi describe herself (Ruth 1:21)?_____

_____

How different our past appears to us in the light of present events. Looking back to the time of famine when she and Elimelech had left Bethlehem, Naomi realized that, despite its problems, it had been a time of "fullness," compared to the emptiness she experienced after her "sojourn" in Moab.

Read **Ruth 1:22.**
(18)  In what season of the year did the women return?_____

_____

The beginning of the barley season would correspond to our early spring.

Read **Deuteronomy 8:7-10.**
In these verses Israel is called among other things a "land of...barley."

(19)  How is it described in verses 9 and 10?_____

_____

_____

_____

_____

Although Naomi did not realize it at the time, the day that seemed so empty to her was the first day of a whole new life for her. This verse from Deuteronomy proved prophetic in her life. The time had begun for both women to eat and be *satisfied*. Afterward, she was able to "bless the Lord [her] God for the good land," which He had given her.

## To Memorize

*Where you go, I will go, and where you lodge, I will lodge. Your people shall be my people, and your God, my God. Where you die, I will die, and there I will be buried (Ruth 1:16b-17).*

# God's Provision

## Introduction

Life could be extremely difficult for a widow in ancient Israel. If she had no sons to care for her, the already husbandless woman was left totally to her own resources, *except for the mercy of God.*

The world often seems not to care, but God, in His infinite mercy, has always cared for society's unwanted: the alien, the stranger, the poor, the orphan, the widow. When God began to prepare the Israelites for their life in the Promised Land, His law included provision for the widow.

*Prayer: Lord, thank You that this story of people who lived thousands of years ago, has, through Your Holy Spirit, the power to change lives today. Let this be so today.*

## Bible Study

Read **Exodus 22:22.**
(1)   What was God's command?_____
(2)   What was the Lord's provision for widows and the needy, as given in these verses?

Deuteronomy 10:18_____

_____

_____

Psalm 146:9_____

Proverbs 15:25_____

Read **Deuteronomy 26:12.**

(3)   What was the Lord's practical provision?_____

_____

_____

**Discussion Question:** Share with your group a time when God has shown His care for you when you were either alone or felt alone.

The idea of caring for the widow and the unfortunate is also at the heart of New Testament Christianity.

Read **Acts 6:1-6.**
(4)    What was the problem indicated in the first verse_____

_____

_____

(5)    How was the problem resolved?_____

_____

Although these verses are concerned with a temporary problem, the fact that it is mentioned and resolved shows that the early Church took seriously God's command to care for the widows and orphans.

Read **1 Timothy 5:2-16.**
(6)    What are these verses concerned with?_____

Read **James 1:27.**
(7)    How does James define "pure and undefiled" religion?_____

_____

_____

Ruth and Naomi, two destitute widows, returned to Bethlehem and, although they probably did not realize it, to the loving, caring arms of the Father.

Once they had arrived, the two women were faced with the very practical necessity of finding a place to live. Since Elimelech planned only a sojourn rather than a permanent stay in Moab, the land that he and Naomi had formerly lived on had probably not been sold. Perhaps Naomi and Ruth returned there. What a sight must have greeted their eyes! After ten years of neglect, any living quarters on the land would undoubtedly have been in a state of disrepair. But Naomi and Ruth were in no position to be fussy. At least, they had some place to live.

Once they were settled, the immediate problem confronting them was the necessity of providing for their basic human needs—food, shelter, warmth.

Read **Ruth 2:2-3.**

17

(8)   What did Ruth suggest?_____
      The practice of gleaning was another of God's provisions for
widows, orphans and other needy people.

Read **Leviticus 19:10** and **Deuteronomy 24:17-24.**
(9)   Describe some of these provisions._____

_____

_____

_____

      Ruth probably would not have been out of order if she had sug-
gested that both she and Naomi go and glean, but the fact that she was
determined to care for the older woman reveals the gentle, loving
heart of this young woman.

Read **Ruth 2:4** and **2:1.**
(10)  In whose field did Ruth glean?_____

(11)  Who was Boaz?_____
      How beautifully the Lord works behind the scenes in the lives of His
people even when we are unaware of it. Of all the fields of Israel Ruth
could have gleaned in, she "happened" to come to a portion of land
belonging to Boaz. There are no coincidences in God.

**Discussion Question:** Relate a time when God has worked behind the
scenes in your life.

Read **Ruth 2:4-7.**
(12)  What did Boaz question the servant in charge of the reapers

      about? _____
      Although there were undoubtedly many reapers in Boaz's field, he
noticed a new face immediately. It is to his credit that he recognized
his workers individually. Whereas many landowners may have only
tolerated the gleaners who followed after the hired men and servants,
Boaz showed his personal interest in those who gleaned in his field.
      By our standards today, the "city" of Bethlehem would be con-
sidered a small village. The early suspicions which most certainly must
have greeted Ruth's arrival had turned to admiration as the townspeo-
ple noted her gentle care and concern for Naomi. Although he had not
previously met her, certainly Boaz would have heard stories about this
Moabitess daughter-in-law who had returned with Naomi.

(13)  What had Ruth asked for?_____

"The little house" where the servant indicated she was sitting when Boaz arrived was most likely a field tent that Boaz had put up for the occasional rest and refreshment of the laborers.

Read **Ruth 2:8-9.**

(14) What advice did Boaz give Ruth?_____

_____

(15) What provision had he made for her?_____

_____

Boaz, the kinsman, is a type of the Lord of the Harvest, Jesus, who by His shed blood on the cross became our "blood" brother. Although farmers in Israel sometimes leased their fields out to others, this was not true of Boaz. Neither did he leave the work entirely to the care of his servants. Rather, he was intimately involved in all the processes of harvesting. Notice how carefully his servant reported all details to his master, even including the conversation he had had with Ruth (v. 6).

We can see in Boaz many different aspects of God's personal caring. Our heavenly Father does not trust others with the ultimate responsibility of our provision and care. He is personally and intimately involved in the lives of each of His children through the ministry of the Holy Spirit.

**Discussion Question:** Can you share a time when God ministered to you in a very personal way?

**Personal Question:** The Lord wants to be able to treat us in the same manner Boaz cared for Ruth. What has been your reaction to His request that you stay in His "field," close to His people? Have you been obedient, or have you considered this to be a restriction of your "rights"? If you wish, share with the others in your group.

Read **Ruth 2:10-13.**

(16) What was Ruth's response to Boaz's kindness?_____

_____

(17) Why did Boaz say he was being so kind to her?_____

_____

_____

(18)  What blessing did Boaz bestow on her?_____

_____

_____

_____

Some commentators believe that scriptures which allude to the wings of the Lord refer back to the wings of the cherubim, which covered the mercy seat of the Tabernacle, and was the place where God met with His people.

(19)  What did Ruth say Boaz had done for her?_____

_____

Sometimes the thing we need most in life is a comforting word.

**Discussion Question:** How does the Lord comfort us? Share a personal experience of a time when the Lord has comforted you.

Read **Ruth 2:14-18.**

(20)  What else did Boaz do for Ruth?_____

_____

The vinegar the workers dipped their bread in was a drink made from unripe grapes. The parched corn referred to in the King James Version, was in reality a type of roasted grain. (Corn is indigenous to North America.) This was much better fare than Ruth could have provided for herself.

That Boaz was a generous master and employer is evidenced by the fact that Ruth ate amply and still had some left.

(21)  How did Boaz instruct his servants?_____

_____

Here, we have further evidence of Boaz's concern for Ruth's welfare. In this, he is a true picture of the Lord's loving protection and care for any of His own. Not only does He surround His children with His protection, He provides something extra as well.

When Ruth returned home to Naomi that night, she took with her not only an ephah (roughly a bushel) of barley, but her "leftovers" from lunch.

Read **Ruth 2:19-23.**

(22)  What did Naomi say when Ruth told her where she had gleaned

that day?_____

_____

(23)  What did Naomi tell Ruth about Boaz?_____

_____

(24)  What advice did Naomi give Ruth?_____

_____

(25)  How long did Ruth glean in Boaz's field?_____

_____

Ruth was obedient to both Boaz and Naomi, staying close to the one who provided her protection and nurture.

## To Memorize

*May the Lord reward your work, and your wages be full from the Lord, the God of Israel, under whose wings you have come to seek refuge (Ruth 2:12).*

# Cleansing

## Introduction

Ruth continued to glean throughout the barley and the wheat season under the protective eyes of Boaz, following his instructions of gleaning only in his fields and staying close to his women servants. We can safely assume that Boaz continued to bless her with extra portions of grain and by allowing her to eat with him and his servants.

*Prayer: Now, Lord, as we move toward the heart of the story, give us discernment to recognize what in particular You would teach each one of us.*

## Bible Study

Read **Ruth 3:1** in the KJV.
(1)  What was Naomi's question to Ruth?_____
    To be at rest! Isn't that what each of us wants? To be able to stop struggling—to cease from our own labors. The problem with most of us in this day and age, however, is that we want rest when we want it and on our own terms. God wants to lead us into His rest, but He will only do it in His own prescribed way. Let us continue on with our study to learn what God's way is.

Read **Read 3:2.**
(2)  What did Naomi remind Ruth of?_____
    The word *kinsman* is a translation of the Hebrew word *ga'al,* one who had the right to redeem the estate of another and to marry his widow in order to raise up an heir in his name.
(3)  Look up the words *redeem* and *redemption* in the dictionary and

    write out their meanings: _____

    _____

    _____

    _____

In the *ga'al* we have another foreshadowing of the Lord Jesus, who by His death and resurrection has shown Himself to be a *redeemer* for lost sinners. Let's see what the Bible says He redeemed us from.

(4)    Write down what the following scriptures say we were redeemed from and/or what we receive in each case.

|  | Redeemed from | Receive |
| --- | --- | --- |
| Gal. 3:13 | _____ | _____ |
| Gal. 4:5 | _____ | _____ |
| Col. 1:13-14 | _____ | _____ |
|  | _____ | _____ |
| Heb. 9:15 | _____ | _____ |
| Titus 2:14 | _____ | _____ |
|  | _____ | _____ |

In order for one man to redeem another in ancient Israel, he must
- have been a near relative
- have had the power to redeem
- have been willing to redeem

How perfectly Jesus meets all of these requirements. By virtue of his spilled blood, He became our blood relative. When we accept Him as the Son of God, He who created the world and everything in it, including us, certainly has the power to redeem us. By His willingness to go to the cross in our behalf, He has shown His willingness to redeem us. Truly, the Lord is the *ga'al* for all people, in all circumstances.

Forgiveness or "remission" of sins means the Holy Spirit is able to work in our lives just as if we had never sinned. But as wonderful as this is, it is not the whole story.

Read **Romans 5:1.**

(5)    What else is achieved in salvation?_____

(6)    What is the dictionary definition of *justification?*_____

_____

_____

Justification in the spiritual sense is much more than remission of sins. When I am justified, it is just-as-if-I had never sinned. Justification is acquittal, plus. If we think in terms of money—when we are redeemed, God pays all our debts. But you can have all your debts paid and still be broke. Justification takes us one step further. Justification is taking all the wealth that is in Christ and putting it in our spiritual bank account, making us spiritual billionaires.

Read **Romans 3:22** and **5:18.**
(7)    Just what is it that God has put into our account?_____

_____

(8)    What else do the following verses tell us about justification?

Romans   3:23-24_____

Romans    3:28_____

Romans  5:1_____

Romans  5:9_____

Romans   8:30_____

Titus   3:7_____

**Discussion Question:** What is the difference between Adam and Eve's condition before they sinned and the position of the Christian?

When He justifies us, God deals with our guilt. Although Adam and Eve were without sin before they sinned, they were not justified. God sees the believer as if he were Jesus. He did not see Adam and Eve in that way.

Read **2 Corinthians 8:9.**
(9)    What does this verse say Jesus did?_____

(10)  Why?_____
Through the grace of Jesus, we are made spiritually rich. This deals with all our condemnation and guilt.
There is still another aspect of sin that must be dealt with, however, and that is the habit and defilement of the sin.

Reread **Ruth 3:2.**
(11)  What did Naomi say Boaz would be doing that night?_____

_____

The threshing floor was on the harvest field. The farmer usually re-

24

mained on the floor all night at this time, to prevent thievery and to catch the night breezes which were essential for winnowing.

The winnowing process by which the grain was separated from the chaff was performed by throwing up the grain against the wind with a shovel, after it had first been trodden down by oxen.

Winnowing was considered too important a job to entrust to others. The Lord of the harvest either performed the job himself or it was done under his supervision. Winnowing speaks of cleansing or separation.

The picture of Boaz winnowing is another picture of our Lord of the Harvest, Jesus. During his ministry John the Baptist gave his prophetic picture of Jesus: "And His winnowing fork is in His hand, and He will thoroughly clear His threshing floor; and He will gather His wheat into the barn, but He will burn up the chaff with unquenchable fire" (Matt. 3:12).

Aren't we happy that the Lord handles this job Himself?

(12)  What did the angel tell Joseph about the Son, Mary would bear?

_____

Jesus did not come just to forgive our sins, but to save us from the habit and defilement of sin, as well.

Read **Ruth 3:3.**

(13)  What was Naomi's first instruction to Ruth?_____

_____

See how beautifully the Lord had set the stage for what followed. In this section of the Book of Ruth, through Naomi's instructions to the young woman, we see a beautiful picture of the Christian's walk toward a closer relationship with Jesus.

Just as Ruth had a wise counselor in Naomi, we have our wise Counselor in the Holy Spirit, whose goal it is to lead us toward an ever-increasing intimacy with our Lord. In the Christian walk we call this progressive work of the Holy Spirit, *cleansing* or *sanctification*. This is a necessary part of our Christian experience. Let's see why.

Read **Psalm 24:3-4.**

(14)  Who may come into the presence of the Lord (stand in His holy

place? _____

_____

If we are going to come into an intimate relationship with the Lord, we must move on from justification and allow the Holy Spirit to do a work of cleansing and sanctification in us. It is true that at salvation we have *legal* righteousness, but God doesn't want just a legal relationship. He wants to bring us into a place of loving fellowship, characterized by *practical* right-standing. Without holiness, no one will see God (Heb. 12:14 KJV).

Cleansing in the Bible is frequently used in connection with the idea of sanctification or a setting apart for God's use. In some cases, the translations are used interchangeably.

The first washing is accomplished when we are reborn in Christ.

(15) Read the following scriptures and write the agent used and what is accomplished in each case.

|  | **Agent** | **Accomplishment** |
|---|---|---|
| Acts 22:16 | | |
| Heb. 9:14 | | |
| Heb. 10:10 | | |
| Heb. 13:12 | | |

These "washings" are all related to our original conversion and baptism.

Baptism here refers to water baptism, a symbolic act in which the believer identifies with Christ in his death, burial and resurrection. There is a continuing work of cleansing which should be going on in the life of the believer after the rebirth experience, *sanctification*.

(16) Read the following scriptures and write the agent of sanctification used in each case.

John 15:3

Acts 26:18

Romans 15:16

1 Corinthians 1:2

1 Corinthians 6:11

Ephesians 5:26

2 Thessalonians 2:13-14

1 Timothy 4:5

1 Peter 1:2

But is all sanctification accomplished by God? What part do we play in the sanctifying process?

(17) Read the following scriptures and see what is required of us.

Acts 26:18_____

1 Timothy 4:4_____

1 Peter 3:15_____

2 Timothy 2:21_____

*The Amplified Bible* translates 2 Timothy 2:21 as
> So whoever cleanses himself (from what is ignoble and unclean)—who separates himself from contact with contaminating and corrupting influences—will (then [himself]) be a vessel set apart and useful for honorable and noble purposes, consecrated and profitable to the Master, fit and ready for any good work.

There is still one more step. What are we to do if we discover sin and disobedience in ourselves?

Read **1 John 1:9-10.**
(18) What is our part?_____

(19) What will God do in return?_____

Read **Romans 3:23.**
(20) Who has sinned?_____

Read **Isaiah 55:7** and **Proverbs 28:13.**
(21) What is our next step, following confession of sin?_____

_____

(22) What happens to the person who tries to hide his sins?_____

_____

Read **Philippians 3:13.**
(23) What are we supposed to do as the final step?_____

Read **Hebrews 8:12** and **10:17.**
(24) What do these verses say about God's attitude toward con-

fessed sin?_____

We must never dwell on past mistakes. It hinders our faith and God's blessing on our life. By forgetting our confessed sin, we are emulating our Father in heaven.

In terms of our story, Naomi has said to Ruth, "Ruth, you have to be washed; you've been saved, but if you're going to have a relationship with Boaz, you need to be washed."

## To Memorize

*Let the wicked forsake his way, and the unrighteous man his thoughts; and let him return to the Lord, and He will have compassion on him; and to our God, for He will abundantly pardon (Isa. 55:7-8).*

# Anointing

## Introduction

We have seen how the story of Ruth can serve as a pattern for the growing or progressive relationship the Christian is to have with the Lord. The first step, Ruth's decision, "Your God shall be my God," is equivalent to the salvation or spiritual rebirth experience. This is followed by Naomi's first instruction to Ruth, "Wash yourself," which speaks of the cleansing from sin and defilement, water baptism and the sanctification by the Holy Spirit. Now, we want to consider the third step in our growing relationship with the Lord.

*Prayer: Dear Lord, how this lovely story of Ruth's faithfulness blesses us and opens our eyes to the kind of personal relationship You are leading us into. Please continue to teach us.*

## Bible Study

Reread **Ruth 3:3.**
(1)  What instruction followed Naomi's charge to Ruth to wash her-

self? _____
Anointing was an ancient custom practiced in eastern countries by most people as a part of their personal grooming. Abstinence in personal anointing was often a sign of mourning. Ruth had probably neglected this part of her grooming as a sign of her mourning for her dead husband and relatives.

The practice was also used in connection with the coronation of kings, the installation of the high priest and as an act of hospitality toward a guest. For these occasions, olive oil, either pure or mixed with perfumes and costly spices, was used.

Oil was also used for healing, for comfort and as a means of illumination. Oil has long been one of the symbols of the Holy Spirit, for He provides anointing, healing, comfort and illumination of God's Word for the believer today.

Read **Acts 2:38.**
(2)  According to the sequence given here, what follows "repent and

be baptized"? _____

_____

If we are going to come into a *full* relationship with the Lord of the Harvest, we cannot consider the baptism in the Holy Spirit as an option, but an essential part of our walk with God.

Read **Acts 1:4-5.**
(3)   What were the disciples commanded to do?_____

_____

(4)   What did Jesus say would happen to them?_____

_____

Read **Ephesians 5:18.**
(5)   What are we told to do in this verse?_____
Both Jesus' and Paul's words were commands. If we are going to have an intimate relationship with the Lord, we are under commandment to be filled with the Holy Spirit. Of course, we don't seek this baptism to satisfy some legalistic requirement. No, God has given us the commandment for our best interest. When He asks us to do certain things, it isn't because He's trying to impose something on us that will deprive us of liberty, privilege or blessing. Rather, He's trying to give us something that will *give* us liberty, privilege and blessing. Obedience to any of God's commands leads us to that end. The Ten Commandments were given to bless the human race, and when we don't obey them, we don't break *them;* they break *us.*

**Discussion Question:** Can you give an example of a time when following one of God's commandments proved to be a specific blessing for you.

"Anoint yourself," Naomi said to Ruth. Let's see God's purposes in the anointing.

Read **Isaiah 10:27** in the KJV.
(6)   What will the anointing do?_____
The word used here for *anointing* means something slightly different from oil poured or rubbed on. It means *fatness.* The very fatness of the land of Israel would break off the yoke of Assyrian bondage, or rather the Lord of Israel would break off the yoke.
Before we come to Christ, we are under a worse bondage than that of Assyria. We are under bondage to Satan. Christ's desire for us is that there be a complete break with this old bondage, our being

"yoked" to Satan and his kingdom.

A yoke was a crossbar with two V-shaped pieces that encircled the neck of a pair of oxen or other animals working in a team. It has long been symbolic of subjugation or bondage. Later in history the Romans forced their conquered enemies to march under a "yoke" made of two upright spears with a third laid across them, as a sign of their subjugation.

In the traditional marriage ceremony there is a vow to *forsake all others*. Likewise, this is one of the ways the Holy Spirit leads us in bringing us to Christ. In salvation, there is the breaking away from the power of darkness and the kingdom of Satan and a releasing to Christ and His Kingdom.

In the cleansing process we see release from the habit and defilement of sin in order that we might be released to Christ in an even fuller dimension. Now we come to anointing. In the scripture in Isaiah, we see the yoke of all our former ties, associations with the old life and any bondage to it can be destroyed by the anointing. Christ's anointing abolishes our former loves in order that we might be married to Him.

**Read Matthew 3:11.**

(7)   What did John the Baptist say Jesus would baptize with?_____

_____

**Read Acts 2:3.**

(8)   What happened on the Day of Pentecost?_____

_____

When we are baptized in the Holy Spirit, the baptism of fire is to burn and consume the remnants of the old life. We are released from the old habits of sin to serve Christ in a fuller dimension.

A friend found weeds in his garden, which he ignored, thinking he would get to them later. Later, when he tried to pull up the weeds, he found they had turned into dry, crusty brambles, and he could not pull the roots out. Furthermore, when he tried, he scattered seeds all over the ground. He now had hundreds of weed seeds all over his flower garden. The only thing he could think of to do was to set fire to all those seeds.

As he was doing this, the Holy Spirit said, "That's what I want to do through the baptism of the Holy Spirit—burn up all the scattered seeds of the former life that would come up and be a blemish in the flower garden of My work in your life."

God applies some fire in the baptism in the Holy Spirit because He wants the whole yoke not only broken, but completely destroyed, the final expression of the old life crushed.

Read **Leviticus 8:30.**
(9)    What did Moses do to Aaron and his sons?_____

_____

   The anointing with oil was part of the consecration services of the priests in the Old Testament.

Read **1 Peter 2:5.**
(10)   What are we being built up as?_____

(11)   For what purpose?_____

_____

   In the Old Testament the anointing related to the priestly ministry. We receive the baptism in the Holy Spirit, that is, our anointing and, with it, a priestly ministry. According to New Testament Scripture, the priestly ministry is not reserved for the clergy; it is the privilege and responsibility of every Spirit-baptized believer.
   Old Testament priests offered up physical (animal) sacrifices. The function of the New Testament priesthood is to offer up *spiritual sacrifices.*

**Discussion Question:** What are spiritual sacrifices?

Read **1 Samuel 10:1.**
(12)   What does Samuel do to Saul in this verse?_____

_____

(13)   Why?_____

Read **1 Samuel 16:13.**
(14)   What are the Lord's instructions to Samuel?_____

_____

_____

(15)   Where was David when Saul reached the house of Jesse?_____

_____

(16)   When the Lord indicated that David was His choice, what did

       Samuel do?_____

(17)   What happened as a result?_____

32

Read **1 Peter 2:9.**

(18)  What does Peter say the Christian is?_____

A race chosen by God. But chosen for what?

(19)  What else does Peter call us?_____

Royal refers to kingly. This is a king who is also a priest and a priest who is also a king. When the Lord comes to anoint us in the baptism in the Holy Spirit, it is for this dual priestly-kingly role.

We have access to God through the finished work of Christ on the cross.

Read **Matthew 27:50-51.**

(20)  What happened in the temple at the moment of Christ's death?

_____

An unseen hand reached down and ripped into two pieces the heavy ornate veil separating the Holy Place from the Holy-of-Holies so that the priests on duty found themselves looking into the very presence of God.

Christ, through His death, had provided access into the very presence of God, access to the mercy seat of God. Now we can go directly into the presence of the living God with our petitions. We can also act as intermediary for the needs of others, bringing their petitions to God in intercession. We are priests unto God.

Through the anointing of the Holy Spirit we are given power and authority, boldness to speak the word of God, the ability to perform signs and wonders. This is the royal anointing, the divine enablement, the ability to express to the outside world what we have learned in the presence of God in our role as priests.

**Discussion Question:** What are some of the other priestly functions? What are some of the kingly functions?

Read **Acts 4:29-31.**

(21)  What did the early Church pray for?_____

_____

_____

(22)  What happened after they had prayed?_____

_____

The result of their prayer was that God did heal, that signs and wonders were done in the early days of Christianity. They did speak the Word of God with boldness.

This scriptural prayer should be prayed by all of us. We need to continually cry out for the ability to express the will of God on this earth and the promised power that comes through His anointing.

We need to make a very important point here. The anointing is a sacred trust given to us to enable us for service as kings and priests unto God. Misuse of the anointing is serious and dangerous and we need to know why.

Satan was an angel of great beauty and perfection. He possessed all of God's good gifts and surely bore the anointing of God upon him. "You were the anointed cherub who covers" (Ezek. 28:14). But then one day unrighteousness was found in him (v. 15) and Satan was deposed by God.

Satan, having known the power of the anointing, will surely try to cause God's children to abuse their anointing. A right relationship, first with the Lord and then with our brothers and sisters in Christ, offers us protection from abuse of the anointing.

God wants us to have both the kingly and the priestly anointing. The kingly anointing is to power; the priestly anointing is to holiness. Both are important for well-balanced Christian living; either without the other is incomplete.

Saul had the kingly anointing without the priestly anointing. He was destroyed by it. He had power without holiness and without holiness he could not control the power.

Solomon had the kingly anointing without the priestly anointing. He multiplied horses and wives, both of which were forbidden in the law. He, too, was destroyed by the kingly anointing without the priestly.

There have been many anointed men who have ministered in this country who have been destroyed by the anointing because they lost the priestly anointing and kept only the power of a kingly anointing.

One of the things God is restoring in this last hour is true holiness. By true holiness, we're talking about the work of the Holy Spirit that penetrates to our very depths. There is the potential in the anointing to bring full release from the power of sin, if we will accept it.

In the Old Testament, we can see this two-fold anointing resting on one person.

**Read Genesis 14:1-20.**

This is the story of Abraham's rescue of his nephew, Lot, from the hands of enemy kings. Lot, we remember, after leaving Abraham, went to live in Sodom. In time Sodom and Gomorrah were attacked and looted. The enemies took Lot captive. When Abraham (then Abram) heard that Lot was a prisoner, he took his trained men and defeated the enemy forces.

(23)  On his way home who met him (v. 18)?_____

(24) Who was Melchizedek?_____

Melchizedek is a shadowy figure of the Old Testament. We know from this verse that he was king of Salem and a priest of God, but he bears no geneology, he seems to be without beginning and without end.

Who is this person who commands such respect from Abraham that he pays him a tenth of all his goods? He is referred to in only one other place in the Old Testament, Psalm 110:4. There God swears to make Someone (his Son) a priest forever according to the order of Melhizedek.

In the New Testament the writer of the Hebrews compares the priesthood of Jesus to the priesthood of Melchizedek. It is, however, a greater priesthood than that of Melchizedek.

Melchizedek is a type of Jesus—both priest and king.

Read **Exodus 19:5-6.**
In the third month after the Children of Israel had left Egypt, God revealed His desire for them.

(25) What did God say they would be if they kept His commandments? _____

_____

God's original purpose was to have a whole nation who would be both kings and priests, as exemplified by the mysterious King of Salem, Melchizedek, but this plan was thwarted by the Israelites.

Read **Exodus 20:18-21.**
(26) What was the people's response to the presence of God?_____

_____

(27) What did they say?_____

_____

The frightened children of Israel, in effect, turned down God's offer to make them a nation of priests—to have God speak to them directly with no mediator standing between them. He then gave the priesthood to one tribe, Aaron and his descendants.

Later, after Israel was settled in the Promised Land, God raised up men upon whom fell the two-fold ministry of both king and priest. These were the judges.

These men and one woman were not judges in the sense we think of a judge today, someone sitting behind a court bench holding a gavel. These were people like Samson, who delivered Israel from the hands of the Philistines, and Deborah, who delivered them from the Canaanites.

God reigned through these judges, so Israel had a kingly ministry without the title and also a priestly ministry without the title. These judges exercised spiritual authority and had access to God. They talked to God and then they went out and did what God wanted done, and they expressed it in a kingly way with power and authority.

Samuel was the last of these judges. When he was a small boy, his mother took him to the high priest for priestly training and there he began to hear the voice of God. Throughout his lifetime, he tried to lead the people in the ways of God, but frequently they didn't listen to him.

Read **1 Samuel 8:4-5.**
(28) What did the people demand of Samuel?_____

_____

Although God, through Samuel, tried to dissuade the people, they would not listen to him and God gave them their way. Thus Saul became king.

The priestly anointing passed to the Levites and the kingly anointing to the kings. In Christ's day the priestly anointing, separated from the kingly anointing, produced a number of sects, among them the Pharisees, who were without any power and put great emphasis on externals and "holiness."

There is good reason to believe that in our day the priestly anointing without the kingly anointing produces legalistic, self-righteousness, "holier-than-thou" groups of exclusive people, devoid of compassion, concern and love for broken, fallen humanity.

Read **Revelation 1:5-6.**
(29) What are we made, according to this verse?_____

_____

(30) Who makes us kings and priests?_____
We need a very heavy mixture of both the kingly and the priestly anointings and we need to be rightly related to the Lord of the Harvest if we're going to fulfill the purposes of God.

Read **Acts 4:29-31.**
(31) Write out the prayer of the Early Church. _____

_____

_____

_____

The scriptural prayer prayed by the early Church should be prayed by all of us. We need to be crying out for the ability to express the will of God in this earth and the promised power that comes through God's anointing.

Reread **Ephesians 5:18.**

**Discussion Question:** If the disciples had been baptized with the Holy Spirit on Pentecost, why did they need to be filled again?

The baptism in the Holy Spirit is not a one-time experience that lasts forever in its impact on our lives or its results. It is not a goal—but a gateway. For every New Testament believer the order is repent, be baptized, receive the gift of the Holy Spirit. But once having experienced the baptism in the Holy Spirit, we need to maintain it every day.

*Do not get drunk with wine,...but be filled with the Spirit.*

The *be filled* in Greek is a present, continuing word. It should be translated as *being filled.*

Too many of us are trying to do the Lord's work with run-down spiritual batteries. The question is: how do we recharge them? The answer is: by speaking in tongues every chance we get—while we're driving, gardening, doing housework, during our lunch break, at work.

God wants to anoint and empower us. He wants to do a work of cleansing and purifying in our hearts. He wants to bring a baptism in the Holy Spirit and of fire to us. The first is on the purifying side of this experience to produce holiness, and He wants the power on the other side so we can go out and do the supernatural work of God. Let us come crying for the double anointing, for the fullness of it, and all that's needed to balance it once it has come.

## To Memorize

*But you are a chosen race, a royal priesthood, a holy nation, a people for God's own possession, that you may proclaim the excellencies of Him who has called you out of darkness into His marvelous light (1 Pet. 2:9).*

# Our Garments

## Introduction

We have been studying the heart of the book of Ruth—how Naomi advises Ruth on what steps to take that will lead her into a deeper relationship with Boaz. We are also seeing how these same steps will bring us into a deeper relationship with our Lord of the Harvest, Jesus.

*Prayer: Oh, Father, how grateful we are for Your caring concern and teaching. How wonderful to know that Your heart's desire is to draw us even closer to You.*

## Bible Study

Reread **Ruth 3:3.**
(1)   What is the next step after the washing and the anointing?____

_____

The King James Version translates this same passage in a much more poetic fashion: "Put thy raiment upon thee."
The Bible has a lot to say about our *clothing.*

## Read **Matthew 22:1-14.**
(2)   What was different about one man at the wedding feast (v. 11)?

_____

(3)   What did the king have done to him?_____

_____

To understand the import of the king's action we have to know that at Eastern weddings the garments worn by the guests were provided for them. Consequently, the man in question, even though he had accepted the invitation that so many had rejected, had refused to wear the wedding garments. In the end he was expelled from the feast.

If our desire is to be in right relationship with our Lord, we must be willing to wear the garments He selects, now and in the future.

Read **Revelation 6:11.**
(4)  With what are the martyred saints provided?_____

Let's look at some of the garments and ornaments the Bible talks about.

Read **Isaiah 52:1.**
(5)  What is Jerusalem commanded to clothe herself in?_____

_____

There is a point in our experience where God begins to want us to put on the right garments for our relationship with Him. We obviously are not talking about external garments or natural garments. These garments referred to in Isaiah deal with spiritual principles we will be discussing.

Read **Isaiah 61:10.**
(6)  What kinds of clothing are mentioned in this verse?_____

_____

Read **Leviticus 8:1-10.**
(7)  What are these verses concerned with?_____

_____

(8)  What do verses 7-9 describe?_____

The priests of the Old Testament were not allowed access into the Holy Place or into the Holy of Holies unless they were wearing the proper garments designated by the Lord. To attempt to do otherwise was presumption and could be punished by death.

**Discussion Question:** Imagine yourself walking into the presence of God. What spiritual garments would you like to be wearing? What would you like to avoid having as part of your spiritual clothing?

At Jesus' death, the heavy curtain separating the Holy of Holies from the rest of the tabernacle was torn in two. By this act God has shown us that we who are Christians have the privilege of coming into the Holy of Holies, into God's very presence where formerly only the High Priest had been allowed to go once a year. Just think what that means! In the past, only one man, once a year had the kind of access we have to God, moment by moment. But just as the High Priest had to meet certain conditions before He could go into the presence of God, so do we. The Bible clearly teaches that if we are to be His priests there needs to be a work of justification in our lives, a work of sanctification, a work of anointing and there are certain garments we must wear. If we are going to live in the presence of God and have a close relationship with Him, we must wear the garments He selects for us.

Let's take a look at the story of another priest in the Old Testament who had to accept the right garments from the Lord.

Read **Zechariah 3:1-6.**

(9) Who was Joshua?_____

(10) How was he dressed?_____

(11) What was the angel of the Lord's command?_____

_____

(12) What was he given to wear?_____

_____

We, too, stand before the Lord as high priests. The Lord has already removed our filthy garments (our sin). Now he requires that we wear the garments of His choice—festal garments and a clean turban.

**Discussion Question:** What might the clean turban symbolize?

Frequently in Scripture, anything related to covering for the head speaks of the mind. We see this same idea expressed in Ephesians.

Read **Ephesians 4:23.**

(13) What is Paul's admonition to us?_____

_____

The clean turban can symbolize the renewed mind.

(14) The Bible also describes other garments selected for us. List the article of clothing or decoration described in the following verses:

Exodus 28:2_____

Leviticus 6:10_____

Proverbs 31:22_____

Proverbs 31:25_____

Ezekiel 44:17_____

Romans 13:12_____

Ephesians 4:24_____

1 Thessalonians 5:8_____

1 Peter 3:3-4_____

A few words of explanation will aid in our understanding: linen in
the Bible speaks of purity. The linen garments were to contain no
wool. Wool would have made the garments warm and would have
caused the priests to sweat. They were not supposed to sweat as sweat
came in with sin and was part of the curse. Man had then to earn his
living by the sweat of his brow, his own effort. So garments of linen
and wool would represent a mixture of God's provision and man's effort. Salvation is a gift of God. There is no effort we can make to ob-
tain it. Purple speaks of royalty.

Read **Psalm 45:13-15.**
(15)  How is the clothing of the King's daughter described?_____

_____

Gold is always a symbol of the diety of God. Part of the clothing the
Lord wants us to wear is godliness or God-likeness. Godliness does
not only refer to God's character but the expression of His powers as
well, as expressed in the fruit of the Spirit.

Read **Galatians 5:22-23.**
(16)  What is the fruit of the Spirit?_____

_____

Read **2 Peter 1:3-4.**
(17)  What are we promised to be partakers of?_____
In the divine nature there is not only the purity of God, but also the
power of God. The two go together. The duty-like qualities woven into our experience are both qualities of God's holiness and qualities of
His power.

Read **Ephesians 6:10-19.**
As priests and kings, we are required to make spiritual war against
our common enemy. For our warfare, God has provided a special
kind of garment or armor.

(18)  Who is our struggle against?_____

_____

(19)  What will this armor enable us to do successfully?_____

_____

(20)  List the pieces of armor and the parts of the body they cover?

_____

_____

_____

_____

_____

Again, all of these pieces of armor are provided by the Lord.

## Read **Luke 15:11-24.**

This is the familiar story of the Prodigal Son and his forgiving father who awaited his return. When the son returned to his home, his father put certain garments on him. Let's take a look at what the father had for his repentent son.

(21)  What kind of robe did the father order the servant to bring?

_____

(22)  What else was he given?_____

The robe the Father provides for us is always the *best* robe. He also provides a ring, which is a symbol of authority, and sandals for our feet, which identifies us as members of the family. (Slaves did not wear sandals.)

There is one garment we will spend the rest of this lesson on.

## Read **Isaiah 61:3.**

(23)  What garment is spoken of here?_____

Of all the garments, this is one the Holy Spirit is particularly emphasizing to us today. If we are ever to have a close relationship with the Lord, we must come into a life of praise and worship.

## Read **John 4:23-24.**

(24)  What is the Father seeking?_____

Apart from the baptism of the Holy Spirit it is just about impossible to have a quality of praise and worship that meets Bible standards.

One thing the baptism in the Holy Spirit does is provide a touch of God upon people's hearts and lives that releases them to a life of praise and worship.

The garment of praise is very important. We must wear it continually, every day until we are able to do as Paul exhorts us: "In everything give thanks for this is the will of God in Christ Jesus concerning you."

It is easy to rejoice when God is giving us a positive blessing, but what about the other times?

Read **Philippians 4:4.**
(25) When does Paul say we should rejoice?_____

God wants our Christian experience to be one of continual, joyful praise, regardless of the circumstances. Too many Christians are like a thermometer that goes up and down with the environment in which it is placed. God calls us to be thermostats. Thermostats control the temperature, the environment.

That's the way praise works in the life of the believer. It controls the environment.

Read **Acts 16:19-26.**
(26) What happened to Paul and Silas?_____

_____

A beating with a cat-o-nine tails was no picnic. A cat-o-nine tails contained sharpened metal barbs so that when it was laid on the back of the victim, it tore away hunks of flesh with every stroke. Every lash of the whipmaster upon a person's back tore out chunks of flesh and muscles. Next, infection would set in with all kinds of complications and problems. Nerves were frequently damaged; and the victims might spend the rest of their lives in excruciating pain.

The Romans laid 39 of these on Paul and Silas before thrusting them into the inner prison where there were no windows or fresh air; furthermore, the men were locked in chains, with their feet in stocks. A guard was appointed to watch them.

Read **Acts 16:25.**
(27) What did Paul and Silas do?_____

**Discussion Question:** Do you think you could have praised God under these circumstances? Give an example of a time when you praised the Lord under adverse circumstances.

(28) What happened after Paul and Silas praised the Lord?_____

_____

_____

That's what can happen when you're wearing a garment of praise.
Remember, we said that God wants us to be thermostats rather than thermometers. The thermostat controls the temperature. Whenever

43

the thermostat senses it's too hot, it shuts down the source of heat; when it senses it's too cold, it turns up the heat to warm the environment.

Praise acts like that in the life of the believer. It controls the environment. When we learn to praise, learn to wear the garment of praise continually, to rejoice evermore, to give thanks in everything, the environment around us is always controlled. Our life is not up and down with the circumstances, but it is a life of praise and worship that controls everything around it.

Let's take a look at one other person who wore a garment of praise.

Read **Job 1:1-3.**
(29) Summarize Job's possessions._____

_____

Read **Job 1:13-19.**
(30) What was taken from Job?_____

_____

Read **Job 1:20.**
(31) What was Job's reaction to this disaster?_____

_____

Many of us probably would have fallen to the ground, but it wouldn't have been because we were worshiping. Many of us would have been complaining, blaming God. Job was different; the Bible tells us that in all of this, Job did not sin with his lips. He put on the garment of praise and worship.

Read **Job 42:10.**
(32) What was the inevitable outcome of Job's attitude of praise?

_____

_____

It was God's mercy to Job that he had learned to wear the garment of praise.

Read **Psalm 100:4.**
(33) How are we to come into the Lord's presence?_____

_____

God's command to us is to come into His courts wearing the garment of praise. We must not come into the Holy of Holies unless we're wearing this garment of praise.

We need to take this garment upon us and learn to praise the Lord, give thanks in everything, rejoice in the Lord always. And when we come to that place when things all around us, from a natural point of view, are falling apart, that's the time we need to praise the Lord. And when things get worse, we praise all the more and the worse things get, the harder we praise. Nothing shakes up the devil more.

## To Memorize

*Giving them a garland instead of ashes, the oil of gladness instead of mourning, the mantle of praise instead of a spirit of fainting...(Isa. 61:3).*

## Lesson Seven

# Getting Down

## Introduction

The Christian's desire must always be to come into an ever closer relationship with our Lord. For the past several lessons we have seen how Naomi's advice to Ruth provides a series of steps that will continuously bring us closer and closer to the One we love and serve.

*Prayer: Lord, it is so wonderful to know that not only have You put this desire for closeness with You into our hearts but that Your Word shows us the way to achieve that closeness.*

## Bible Study

Reread **Ruth 3:3** in the KJV.
(1)   What is the step following the putting on of the garments?____

_____

Getting down to the floor speaks of two things: first, getting to a place where the Lord can work with us and, second, entering into a life of communion with Him.

Read **Matthew 11:28.**
(2)   Who does Jesus invite us to come to?_____

It is important that we understand this point clearly. Jesus' first call to every person is "to come to Me," not to Africa, not to South America, not the slums of New York City or not even Timbuktu. His first call is always to come to Himself.

It is after we have come to Him that He sends us out—after we have established an intimate relationship with Him, after we have taken His yoke and received His strength. When we go out in our own zeal, the enemy can pick us off like flies. Why? Because we haven't learned God's ways. We haven't taken time to establish a relationship with Him. The point is, the work of the Kingdom is going to be done by men and women who have a relationship with the Lord of the Harvest.

We must set aside time, to get to know Him, to come to the place where He can work with us.

Read **Acts 13:47.**
(3)    What had the Lord told Paul?_____

_____

The Lord possibly told Paul this on the day of his conversion; yet it was 14 or 15 years of learning to walk with God before Paul was sent out to minister extensively. That word of the Lord did not find its expression in Paul until many years later—after he had had time to establish a relationship with the Lord of the Harvest.

Read **Isaiah 4:1.**
(4)    What do the seven women want from the man?_____

_____

(5)    What will they continue to do?_____

_____

This is the story of too many Christians today. They say, "Lord, we'll eat our own bread and we'll wear our own clothes. Just give us Your name—*Christian.*" They aren't interested in a marriage relationship—they only want His name so that their reproach will be taken away.
    However, the purpose for which God saves us is to bring us to Himself in a love relationship.

Read **Matthew 22:36-37.**
(6)    What was the lawyer's question to Jesus?_____

_____

(7)    What was Jesus' answer?_____

_____

Read **Deuteronomy 10:12.**
(8)    What does God require of us?_____

_____

_____

    In our relationship with the Lord, the right order is to love Him first—then serve Him.

Read **Luke 10:38-42.**
(9)    Why did Jesus refuse to rebuke Mary?_____

The "good part" is to spend time at Jesus' feet *before* we attempt to serve Him.

**Personal Question:** If you were to evaluate your relationship with the Lord, how would you label yourself—a Mary or a Martha?

If we are not spending considerable time in prayer, both listening and speaking to God each day, we need to re-evaluate our priorities.

The second thing getting down to the floor speaks of, is coming down to a place of brokenness, contriteness and humility.

Read **Psalm 138:6.**
(10)  What does this scripture say about God?_____

_____

The Lord can never fellowship with a proud spirit. God has to work pride out of us, possibly more than any other sin.

Getting down to the floor implies letting God deal with the pride in our lives. Pride is not the same as self-esteem, but rather a cover-up for the absence of it. Pride is making ourselves something we are not, to try to cover up our lack of inward assurance that we are people with value, to make us acceptable to God and men.

The answer to pride is having a pure relationship between God and ourselves. Being secure about ourselves and about God is really God's answer to pride. God comes to work in our hearts over and over again, to bring us to the place where we trust Him implicitly. We don't need a facade; we can be confident and relaxed in our relationship with Him. This is the balance that God brings us to, a life where we realize we're valuable to God—so valuable He died for us.

Read **Psalm 34:18.**
(11)  Who does the Lord come near?_____

(12)  Whom does He save?_____
The "crushed in spirit" is translated *contrite* in the KJV.

The Lord sees the proud from afar and He keeps them there. He will not allow pride in His presence. It was Satan's pride that caused his downfall. God hates pride. He will not tolerate it in the life of His children.

Read **Psalm 51:17.**
(13)  What does God look favorably upon?_____

_____

Read **Song of Solomon 1:9.**

48

(14)   What does this scripture compare the believer with?_____

_____

In this verse the believer is compared to one of those ten or fifteen horses that pulled Pharoah's chariot. Those horses had tremendous spirit, but they had been "broken." When a horse is broken, he will accept the bridle and saddle on the harness. With proper training he will come under perfect obedience, but he still has spirit. He can pull a chariot with great pomp, and yet at the least little tug on the rein the horse immediately responds, turning right or left, stopping, proceeding quickly or slowly as commanded. A properly trained horse is a joy to work with.

He's completely different from a zebra. Some missionaries once tried to break zebras the way one breaks horses. There was one big problem. When the zebra was broken, he was completely without spirit. He just lay down and wanted to die. Some people are like that when God disciplines them.

**Read Jeremiah 17:9.**
(15)   Why is it necessary for God to break the human heart or spirit?

_____

_____

**Read Isaiah 57:15.**
(16)   Who will God dwell with?_____
  The word *contrite* means the same as *broken.*
(17)   What does God say He does to the spirit of the lowly and the

  contrite heart?_____
  If we want God's presence and revival, the way is through a contrite and lowly spirit. Why does God live with those with a humble, broken and contrite spirit? Because that is His nature. His is not a proud spirit.

**Read James 3:14.**
(18)   What does God tell us to do about bitter jealousy and selfish

  ambition? _____

**Read Proverbs 13:10 in the KJV.**
(19)   What causes contention?_____
  Behind all strife, bitterness and envy is pride—undealt with pride.

**Read James 3:17-18.**

(20)   What is the wisdom that comes from God?_____

_____

_____

Because God is a humble, broken and contrite spirit, whenever He manifests His wisdom, it is always a manifestation of those qualities that come forth in purity, peace, gentleness, reasonableness, full of mercy and good fruits, unwavering, without hypocrisy. That's the kind of spirit that He is. And so when it is His Spirit at work, that's what is manifested.

When we move in the utterance gifts (tongues, interpretation, prophecy), there is a great need for God to deal with our spirits, that they be broken, contrite and humble.

Read **Isaiah 66:2.**
(21)   To whom will God look?_____

_____

God says in effect, "I won't look to heaven and earth and all those things that I made; I'm going to watch and look and be with the man that is poor and of a contrite spirit and trembles at (has high regard for) any word from God, so much so that he's like the trained horse. The gentlest impression of the Holy Spirit and he immediately responds, 'Yes, Lord.'"

Read **Psalm 32:8.**
(22)   How does God want to counsel (guide) us?_____
A teacher related that in working with children with learning disabilities, she discovered they frequently do not respond to symbols, such as a look from the teacher, a direction given by the eye, etc. Aren't a lot of us like that? We have learning problems, and so God can't direct us with just a signal from His eye.

Read **Psalm 32:9.**
(23)   When God is not able to guide us with His eye, what does He

use? _____
If you belong to God, He is going to guide you one way or the other. How would you prefer Him to do it—with His eye or with the bit and bridle?

## To Memorize

*The Lord is near to the brokenhearted, and saves those who are crushed in spirit (Ps. 34:18).*

# Resting

## Introduction

We have been studying the steps of coming into a more intimate relationship with our Lord of the Harvest, Jesus, through the example given in the book of *Ruth.*

*Prayer: Lord, it is our heart's desire to come into a closer, more intimate relationship with You. Please speak to our spirits through this study today.*

## Bible Study

Read **Ruth 3:3-4.**
(1)   What is Ruth to wait for?_____

_____

(2)   What is she to do next?_____
There was nothing improper in Naomi's directions to Ruth. In the time of the book of Ruth, men and women slept fully clothed. A servant usually slept at his master's feet.

Notice that Ruth was instructed to wait until Boaz was alone. Though it is possible to commune with the Lord in the presence of others, there are certain times of intimacy that are only possible with Him alone.
(3)   What is Ruth to do after she learns where Boaz is sleeping?

_____

_____

After she is lying down, then "He [Boaz] will tell you what to do. He will give you guidance," Naomi was telling Ruth.

The problem with most of us is that we want guidance immediately. But we really aren't ready for divine guidance until we have washed, anointed, and clothed ourselves and gone down in humility to the Lord of the Harvest. We are not ready to be used and directed by the Lord until we have been through the preliminary preparation. Many people who have difficulty in receiving guidance have never taken the steps necessary for receiving it.

When you have taken the necessary steps, then God's word will come to you, guiding and directing your life. But there is yet one other step left to take before we can receive guidance. That is to lie down—to be at rest. It's almost impossible for God to guide someone who is uptight, frustrated and shook up. That is why we need to be at rest.

In one of the most poignant scriptures in the Bible, Jesus reveals Himself as the One who can give us the rest we seek.

Read **Matthew 11:28-29.**

(4)  Whom did Jesus address?_____

(5)  What did He promise?_____

(6)  How do we find that rest?_____

Before we become Christians, we are yoked to Satan. The Jews in a very real sense were yoked to the Law and all of its demands. At salva n Jesus puts His yoke on us. The picture given here refers to the practice of yoking oxen together. When a young ox was trained, it was first yoked to an experienced mature ox. As long as he cooperated with the lead ox,  he could work with little strain, the older, stronger ox doing most of the work. However, resisting or fighting the yoke or the direction indicated by the more experienced ox produced only strain and discomfort. The lead ox in the picture is, of course, Jesus.

The second requirement for rest—learning of Him requires our deliberately taking time for prayer, meditation, Bible reading and studying. This is how we learn of Jesus.

**Discussion Question:** Share with your group whether you are resting by moving in union with Jesus or are you fighting against Him?

**Personal Question:** Have you kept your part of the agreement with Jesus? Do you do everything possible to learn about Him? If your answer is no, what are you going to do about it?

Too often we've tended to fire up people by talking about all the lost souls needing to be saved. But before we can become effective soul winners, we have to experience some of the dealings of God and pass through some of these tests.

There comes a point literally of spiritual, physical and mental relaxation where we've come to rest before we can enter into guidance, a place where we can learn to enter into a rest in God about the things that keep shaking us up and down. When we come to a place of committal in putting it all in the hands of God, then God, out of that rest, begins to work. It is the one who has come to this place of quietness in

His presence to whom God can speak.

Read **Read Isaiah 28:16** in the KJV.
(7)    What does this verse say about the person who believes in God's

cornerstone?_____

Read **Proverbs 19:2.**
(8)    What does this verse say about being in haste?_____

_____

Read **Proverbs 29:20.**
(9)    How does the Bible describe a person who speaks hastily?

_____

There's always a hastiness in man's spirit. We're always trying to
run ahead of God and He has to throw up road blocks to slow us
down, stop us, long enough to talk to us and get us oriented and going
the right way.

Read **Hebrews 4:1-12.**
(10)   Who is our example of being at rest?_____

(11)   What has He promised (v. 9)?_____

(12)   What should we fear (v. 1)?_____

The rest we're talking about is an attitude of heart and soul. Some
of the purposes of God require years of preparation to find expression
in our lives. Sometimes when we go ahead of God, we sense that He's
got chains on us and we're dragging balls of His divine apprehension
along. We try to escape some of the things God wants us to go
through. We keep trying to run ahead of God; He continually throws
up roadblocks and we keep crashing into them. He blows out our
tires, He shoots out our radiators. All the time He's trying to get us
stopped long enough to talk to us and get us oriented and going the
right way.

We're talking about coming to a place where we're willing to let
Him start working it all out. Abraham had to come to rest. Sarah had
to come to rest. They had the promises of God, and they had them for
over twenty-five years before they saw anything happen.

God's will has to work itself out in our lives, and it only works out
when we come to rest. When Abraham and Sarah quit trying to work
it out, then God started working, and He worked it out in the birth of
Isaac.

Read **Zechariah 4:6.**

(13) How does God accomplish His will?_____

_____

We have to come to the point where we're going to let the Lord work it out, not by human energy but by divine power. It's letting the power source shift from human to divine ability. When God's power is driving the thing, it's quite a bit different from when we're driving it.

Reread **Hebrews 4:1-12.**

Verse 6 tells that because those others did not enter into rest, God talks about another day through David, saying, "Today, if you'll hear His voice, harden not your heart."

(14) What does verse 9 tell us?_____

_____

(15) How do we enter God's rest?_____

_____

(16) Why were many denied entering His rest?_____

(17) What does verse 12 tell us about God's Word?_____

_____

_____

If we enter into rest, God will bring His Word to begin working in the situation. And His Word is living and powerful; it will get the job done. What you can't do by your work and struggling, God will accomplish. But God's Word doesn't begin to work until we come to a place of rest.

When we rest, the Word of God starts rising up and begins to work and we are ready for the next step. "He will show you what to do."

## To Memorize

*Come to Me, all who are weary and heavy-laden, and I will give you rest (Matt. 11:28).*

## Lesson Nine
# Guidance

## Introduction

Naomi has carefully shown Ruth the steps necessary to come into an intimate relationship with Boaz, the Lord of the Harvest, who represents for us, our Lord of the Harvest, Jesus.

*Prayer: Lord, how grateful we are that You have opened the eyes of our understanding through this Bible study and shown us some of the wonderful secrets that are hidden in Your Word. Continue to guide us from now on into an even greater understanding of what You are teaching us today.*

## Bible Study

Read **Ruth 3:4.**
(1)    What did Naomi say would be the result of Ruth's obeying her

instructions?_____
Isn't that the cry of every Christian's heart? We all want to know what the Lord wants us to do.

**Personal Question:** Receiving guidance from the Lord is the result of walking closely with Him. Have you been willing to take the steps necessary to hear from the Lord.

(2)    What was the step before this one?_____
We are not ready for guidance until we have come to a place of rest. We are not ready to be used and directed by the Lord until we have been through the whole process. Most Christians who seek guidance have not taken the steps necessary to receiving guidance. When we take the steps of guidance, we will find God's Word coming to us and directing our lives.

Read **Ruth 3:5.**
(3)    What was Ruth's response to Naomi's counseling?_____

_____

_____

**Personal Question:** Often we seek advice or counsel, but if the word is difficult, we refuse to follow it. When you go to someone for advice, do you usually follow their advice?

Read **Ruth 3:6-9.**
(4)    Did Ruth follow Naomi's advice in every detail?_____
   How patiently she must have waited for exactly the right moment! Finally, the harvest festivities were ended, and Boaz went to sleep.

(5)    What did Ruth do?_____
_____

(6)    What happened in the middle of the night?_____
_____

(7)    What did Ruth request of him?_____
   To spread a mantle or skirt over someone in the East was to put them under your protection. By her request, Ruth was asking Boaz to make her his wife. We see this same idea expressed elsewhere in the Bible.

Read **Ezekiel 16:1-8.**
(8)    To whom is God through the prophet sharing His words?
_____

(9)    What is the first thing God did for Jerusalem (v. 6-7)?_____
_____

(10)   What else did He do for her (v. 8)?_____
_____

   Here, in God's rebuke to Jerusalem, we see this same symbolism expressed. Describing Jerusalem as a young woman, the Lord said He put His skirt over her—that is, He took her under His protection and claimed her for His own.
   We, too, as spiritual Israelites can ask God to spread His mantle over us.

**Discussion Question:** Have you appropriated this covering and protection of God for yourself?

Read **Ezekiel 16:9.**

(11)  What other similarities can you see between Naomi's suggestions

to Ruth and the Lord's actions toward Jerusalem?_____

_____

Read **Ruth 3:10-11.**
(12)  What was there about Ruth that had particularly pleased Boaz?

_____

**Discussion Question:** Why do you think this would please Boaz?

Ruth's life had not been easy since she had come to Israel. If she had been less the person she was, she could have left Naomi to fend for herself while she sought a new husband among the young men.

Read **Ruth 3:10-13.**
(13)  How did Boaz respond to Ruth's request?_____

_____

(14)  Unfortunately, there was one problem in the way. What was

that  obstacle?_____

In the working out of the leverite law, the closest relative had the right of redemption first.

Read **Ruth 3:14-18.**
(15)  Summarize what happened next._____

_____

(16)  What was Naomi's suggestion when she returned home?_____

_____

(17)  When did Naomi think Boaz would take action?_____
Waiting is not difficult when we have learned to rest and to have perfect trust in the one we are waiting on. Anyone who has truly entered into the Lord's rest is at peace.
Naomi's counsel reminds us of David's attitude expressed in many of the psalms.

Read **Psalm 37:7.**
(18)  What is the psalmist's word to us in this verse?_____

Read **Ruth 4:1-6.**

(19) When did Boaz proceed to handle the problem?_____

Naomi was right in her estimation of Boaz's character. A man of honor, he could not rest until he had carried out his responsibility toward Ruth.

(20) Where did Boaz go?_____

In ancient times, the city gate was a roofed structure with no walls, where all business transactions were made.

(21) Who did Boaz meet there?_____

(22) Whom did he invite to sit with them?_____

All matters of law required witnesses. If the matter were of little consequence, two or three witnesses were sufficient, but for important matters, ten witnesses were required. Boaz, in the presence of witnesses, spelled out the situation concerning Naomi's land.

(23) What was the relative's first response?_____

(24) Why did he change his mind?_____

_____

(25) What did he tell Boaz to do?_____

Read **Ruth 4:7-10.**

(26) How was the deal consumated?_____

_____

(27) How is this custom explained?_____

_____

_____

(28) According to verse 9 and 10, list what Boaz redeemed?_____

_____

_____

Read **Ephesians 5:25.**

(29) What action did Christ take toward the church?_____

_____

Like Boaz, Jesus Christ is the Kinsman-Redeemer who paid for his bride, the Church, at Calvary. When Jesus said, "It is finished," it was a sign the redemption was complete. The sandal had been drawn off.

He waits only for the proper moment to claim His bride. Then He will take her to His home to be with Him forever.

We, who are redeemed by Christ, make up His bride and should be looking for His coming for us. The transaction making the marriage valid has already been completed; we wait now for the wedding day. Neither He nor we will be completed until we are at last united at that heavenly wedding banquet of Christ.

Read **Revelation 19:7-8.**

The marriage of the Lamb is a future, end-time event.

(30)  What similarities do you see between Ruth's preparation for her

bridegroom and that of the Church for Christ?_____

_____

_____

(31)  What does the Church's fine linen represent?_____

_____

Read **Ruth 4:11-12.**

(32)  What was the blessing the witnesses gave?_____

_____

_____

_____

_____

_____

Rachel and Leah were the wives of Jacob, who by their fruitfulness established the house of Israel. Perez, son of Judah, through Tamar is directly in the lineage of Jesus.

It is interesting to note that after this point in the story, Ruth is never again referred to as a Moabitess, reminding us once again that when we are betrothed to Christ, our background or past is completely forgotten.

Read **Ruth 4:13.**
(33) What was the result of this union?_____

The name *Ruth* means "satisfied" and upon her marriage to Boaz and the birth of this child, she became fully satisfied.

Read **Ruth 4:14.**

Naomi's life had come full-circle. She who was called "Pleasant," went out to Moab where she was turned into a bitter old woman. But God blessed her with a daughter-in-law who loved her and was obedient to her counsel. The end result was Ruth's marriage to Boaz and then this child, ancester of kings, Obed.

(34) What was the blessing of the women of Bethlehem upon Naomi?

_____

_____

_____

Read **Ruth 4:16-22.**
(35) How was Obed related to King David?_____

Our story truly has a happy ending. Ruth lived the rest of her life as a fulfilled and fruitful Israelite matron. Boaz, who was willing to raise up a son to another man, nevertheless, is named in Jesus' geneology, given in both Matthew and Luke, as the father of Obed.

Naomi who had returned to Bethlehem bitter and empty now had her arms and heart filled with the grandchild, Obed, who became one link in the direct lineage of Jesus.

## To Memorize

*(1)   Let us rejoice and be glad and give the glory to Him, for the marriage of the Lamb is come and His bride has made herself ready (Rev. 19:7-8).*

*(2)   And the Spirit and the bride say, "Come." And let the one who hears say, "Come." And let the one who is thirsty come; let the one who wishes take the water of life without cost (Rev. 22:17).*